HOUGHTON MIFFLIN GUIDE SERIES

An Educator's Guide to
Inclusion

Kristin L. Sayeski
University of Virginia

James M. Cooper, Series Editor
University of Virginia

HOUGHTON MIFFLIN COMPANY   BOSTON   NEW YORK

Senior Sponsoring Editor: Sue Pulvermacher-Alt
Senior Development Editor: Lisa Mafrici
Editorial Associate: Sara Hauschildt
Manufacturing Manager: Florence Cadran
Marketing Manager: Nicola Poser

Printed in the U.S.A.

ISBN: 0-618-31323-0

89-CRS-09

CONTENTS

PREFACE

Houghton Mifflin Company publishes outstanding education textbooks in the areas of foundations of education, introduction to education, educational psychology, special education, and early childhood education. These textbooks introduce students to many concepts, policies, and research that undergird educational practice. However, as is the case for virtually all introductory texts, many topics are introduced but not covered in great depth. The Houghton Mifflin Teacher Education Guide Series is designed to provide more in-depth coverage of selected educational topics studied in the teacher education curriculum.

At the present time there are five guides in the series:

- Diversity in the Classroom

- Classroom Assessment

- Inclusion

- Technology Tools

- School-based Interventions

The topics for these guides were selected because they are addressed in virtually all teacher education programs, and contain vital information for beginning teachers if they are to be successful in the classroom. Instructors may use the guides either for required or enrichment reading.

Each of these guides provides pre-service teachers with greater in-depth knowledge, application suggestions, and additional resources on its particular topic. All the guides share a common format that includes an introduction to the topic, knowledge that the prospective teacher should possess about the topic, examples of and suggestions for how the knowledge can be applied, and both print and Web-based resources for further exploration. Each guide also contains 10-15 questions designed to help the prospective teacher reflect on the concepts and ideas introduced in the guide, as well as a glossary of key terms.

In this guide on inclusion, author Kristin Sayeski examines the controversy within the special education community on the pros and cons of full inclusion. She defines what inclusion is and is not, presents the legal basis from which the inclusion of students with disabilities in regular education classrooms stems, and provides helpful suggestions on how to implement inclusion successfully. She examines one of these strategies, collaborative or co-teaching, in some detail, including identifying several models of co-teaching, along with practical tips for making co-teaching work. After reading this guide, prospective teachers will have a much greater understanding of the philosophy behind the inclusion movement, along with many ideas of how to accommodate students with disabilities in the regular classroom.

PART I: INTRODUCTION

INCLUSION

One cannot go very far in the field of education and not be confronted with the topic of "inclusion." School districts, individual schools, and even school personnel such as teachers, principals, and parents align themselves along pro-inclusion or anti-inclusion tracks. Frequently framed as a polarizing issue, inclusion is actually a philosophical approach to the instruction of students with disabilities—not an either/or educational proposition. Yet, inclusion remains a controversial issue in education. Part of the controversy stems from the complexity involved in making educational decisions that take into account both academic and social goals. The other component stems from misunderstandings of the concept itself and special education laws related to it. To fully understand the nuances of inclusion (not just popular sentiment), inclusion is best broken down into two categories: what it is not and what it is.

Inclusion—What It Is Not

To start, inclusion is *not* simply the placement of all students with disabilities in **general education settings**. When school districts or principals describe their model of instruction for students with disabilities they will state, "We believe in or endorse inclusion for students with disabilities" or "We are an inclusive school/district." Does this mean that all students with disabilities will spend all of their time in general education settings in those schools? Probably not. Given the diversity of needs and services it is more likely that in those schools or districts most students with disabilities will be spending more time in general education settings than students with disabilities in districts or schools that do not publicly endorse inclusion.

Secondly, inclusion is *not* a moral mandate. Some teachers, advocates, or administrators imply that anyone not for "inclusion" is for "exclusion"—the systematic isolation of students with disabilities from students without disabilities. The logic is this: If inclusion means

1

placement in general education classes, then anti-inclusion would mean placement in separate classes. The lack of middle ground inherent in this argument does not reflect current practices or legal standards. Framing the issue of inclusion as an ethical one polarizes the discussion of instruction for students with disabilities into two possible avenues—one that is "right" and one that is "wrong." Determining what is best for an individual student necessitates the availability of a range of options.

Finally, inclusion is *not* a mandate from the federal government. In fact, the term "inclusion" does not appear in the statute (Individuals with Disabilities Education Act, IDEA) or in the accompanying regulatory standards. Federal legislation *does* call for the placement of students with disabilities in the **least restrictive environment (LRE)**. The LRE for an individual student is the most appropriate educational placement that is closest to instructional environments of students without disabilities. That is, the LRE is unique for each student and for each unique condition the student will encounter. For example, a student may be placed into general education settings for mathematics, science, social studies, lunch, and art but receive reading instruction in a special education classroom. In conjunction with the LRE mandate, federal law requires that a **continuum of alternative placements** be available for students. The continuum includes placement options that range from general education classrooms in the neighborhood school to **resource rooms**, self-contained classes, special day schools, residential or hospital settings, and home instruction. Any of these placement options may be considered the LRE for an individual student.

How is a separate classroom or residential setting considered "least restrictive"? The courts interpret restrictiveness in terms of the student's ability to make appropriate instructional gains and a teacher's ability to instruct the student in such a way that allows for progress and does not hinder the progress of other students. Refer to the box "A Closer Look: The Law and LRE" for summaries of seminal LRE court cases.

A Closer Look   The Law and LRE

Least restrictive environment (LRE) is defined under the Individuals with
Disabilities Education Act (PL 101-467) as:

> *To the maximum extent appropriate, children with disabilities,
> including children in public or private institutions or other care
> facilities, are educated with children who are not disabled, and special
> classes, separate schooling, or other removal of children with
> disabilities from the regular educational environment occurs only
> when the nature or severity of the disability of the child is such that
> education in regular classes with the use of supplementary aids and
> services cannot be achieved satisfactorily.* (5)(a)

Thus, congressional preference is that students with disabilities be placed in
general education settings. The caveat to this preference is when
"education…cannot be achieved satisfactorily." What constitutes "education"
and "satisfactory achievement" is left to individual school districts to
determine. **Case law** and the judicial decisions that result from it provide
necessary guidance in how to act in ways that meet this broad standard. Two
examples of case law decisions that have influenced future LRE cases follow.

Daniel R. R. v. State Board of Education 874 F.2nd 1036 (Fifth Circuit 1989)
Daniel, at the time of litigation, was a 6-year-old boy with Down Syndrome.
His parents had enrolled him in a half-day, special education pre-kindergarten
class and a half-day, general education pre-kindergarten class. Shortly after he
started school, the placement committee determined that Daniel would be better
served in the special education class with only lunch and recess with general
education students. In the general education class, Daniel's teacher reported
that he required almost constant, individualized attention, and he failed to
master any of the skills the other students were working on. In addition, the
school believed that the teacher was spending a disproportionate amount of
time with Daniel at the expense of other children in the room. Daniel's parents
disagreed with the placement decision and the case went to a hearing officer.
The hearing officer agreed with the schools and felt that the teacher would have
to make significant **modifications** to the curriculum for Daniel to yield any
benefit. The case eventually went to the U.S. Court of Appeals for the Fifth
Circuit.

The Fifth Circuit Court devised a two-part test to determine if the schools had
met the LRE standard. Part I asked: Could education, with the use of
supplementary aids and services, be satisfactorily achieved? Part II examined:
If the answer to part one was "no," had the schools included Daniel to the

A Closer Look   The Law and LRE

maximum extent possible? The court decided that given the amount of time the teacher needed to spend with Daniel and the opportunities Daniel would receive to interact with students without disabilities during non-academic times, the school had met the two part standard.

Sacramento City Unified School District v. Rachel H. 14 F.3d 1398 (Ninth Circuit 1994)

In the case of Rachel H., an 11-year old girl with moderate mental retardation, the parents requested full-time placement in the general education setting. The school denied their request and offered to place Rachel in special education settings for academic periods and general education settings for all non-academic periods. The parents enrolled Rachel in a private school while appealing the school's decision. At the **due process hearing**, the hearing officer determined that the schools had not made sufficient effort to include Rachel in general education settings prior to making their determination. The school district appealed to the district court.

The district court agreed with the hearing officer. A four-part test devised to guide them in their ruling asked the following questions:

   a.   What are the educational benefits of the general education placements (with supplementary aids and services) compared with special education placements?

   b.   What are the nonacademic benefits to the children in terms of their interaction with nondisabled peers?

   c.   What are the effects of the children's presence on the general education teacher and nondisabled students?

   d.   What is the cost involved in providing supplementary aids and services in the general education setting?

The court sided with the parents and determined that the educational benefits afforded to Rachel in the general education class were the same as or exceeded the benefits afforded to her in the special education setting. In addition, communication and social benefits could be provided in the general education setting. The courts further found that the cost to the district was not prohibitive nor was the amount of time required by the general education teacher to support Rachel's education. On appeal to the U.S. Court of Appeals for the Ninth Circuit, the court upheld the district's ruling. (Boyle & Weishaar, 2001)

In summary, LRE determinations should be made on an individualized basis. The courts, in interpreting congressional intent, will look to a good faith effort

A Closer Look	The Law and LRE

on the part of schools to make sure placement in general education settings is not feasible prior to the removal of a student with disabilities from general education settings. More restrictive placement options are acceptable if schools have met the initial standard.

Inclusion—What It is

What *is* inclusion, then? Inclusion is a philosophical orientation about the education, employment, and livelihood of people with disabilities. Inclusion stems from the belief that individuals with disabilities are a part of society and as such should be "included" in all aspects of society. Although this concept may be taken for granted today, only recently were individuals with disabilities systematically excluded from society. For example, children born with disabilities often were taken away from their parents, groups of individuals with disabilities were forced to live in institutions or on the outskirts of town, and school-age children with disabilities were not allowed to attend school. Unfortunately, remnants of these exclusionary practices remain today. Exclusion, although not legal, can still be found in the areas of employment, housing, public accommodations, education, transportation, communication, recreation, health services, voting, and access to public services.

Advocates of inclusion, then, believe that the default placement of a person with a disability is as a meaningful participant in all aspects of society. In the educational arena, inclusion means the default placement of a student with a disability is in general education settings. In fact, most controversies surrounding inclusion revolve around the issue of what those specific conditions should be that would necessitate a more restrictive setting. (Refer to the box "A Closer Look: Mainstreaming vs. Inclusion" for how the philosophy of inclusion has changed both language and practice.)

| A Closer Look | Mainstreaming vs. Inclusion |

From an outsider's perspective the language of special education appears to be constantly changing. Cynics dismiss the changes as "political correctness gone awry," but those close to the issues understand that the alteration in language reflect changes in practices, attitudes, and outcomes.

One example of a powerful language change is the substitution of the term "inclusion" for the term "mainstreaming." The concept of mainstreaming came about in the early days of special education. Post Public Law 94-142 (the original special education legislation passed in 1975 that preceded IDEA), schools prepared special classrooms for students with disabilities who would now grace their doorsteps. As educators learned more about this new population of students, they began to see the educational and social advantages to "mainstreaming" students with disabilities into general education classes. **Mainstreaming**, therefore, came to mean the act of moving a student from his or her restrictive setting to the less restrictive setting of the general education classroom for a designated period.

Inclusion, in contrast, means that the "home base" of a student with a disability is in general education settings and that students will move into more restrictive environments as determined by student need. Although some educators continue to use the terms mainstreaming and inclusion interchangeably, they have different meanings and reflect different perspectives about the education of students with disabilities.

INCLUSION DEFINED

What then does inclusion mean for the education of students with disabilities? **Inclusion** is best defined as the commitment to educate students with disabilities in the least restrictive environment. This commitment extends to educating students in the schools they would typically attend if they did not have a disability. Inclusion also means a commitment to bringing support services to students rather than students coming to services. The benefits of inclusion extend beyond the potential for a student with a disability to learn a discrete set of skills. Refer to the box "A Closer Look: Benefits of Inclusion" on page 7 for a list of potential benefits.

People who promote inclusion fall somewhere on a continuum of beliefs about what it means in practice. At one end of the continuum,

A Closer Look   *Benefits of Inclusion*

Potential benefits to be gained from including students with disabilities into general education settings include:

- special education students remain with their peers and are more likely to be integrated into the daily activities of schools;

- general education students gain from their associations with students with disabilities as they learn more about social, cognitive, and emotional differences of others, they also learn more about themselves;

- general education teachers benefit from working with and learning instructional techniques from special educators and related service personnel; and

- special educators benefit from gaining access to general education curriculum and working in contexts that offer a range of positive interactions for students with disabilities. (Lewis & Doorlag, 1999)

some groups advocate for **full inclusion**—all students with disabilities placed in general education settings in neighborhood schools all the time. At the other end of the continuum, people tend to be more favorable of pullout, resource rooms, or separate settings for students with disabilities.

Who does not support inclusion? Those who truly have an anti-inclusion orientation believe that children with disabilities cannot be successful in general education settings even when provided with appropriate supports. Additionally, they argue that the default placement of a child with a disability will be a separate educational setting (e.g., *all* students with mental retardation belong in separate education classes). Few people involved in education will fall into this category; the majority of educators find themselves somewhere on the inclusion continuum.

In summary, it is best to think of inclusion as a starting place—a student with a disability learning side-by-side with a student without a disability. Where you go from there will depend upon the specific educational goals established and the skills and needs of that student.

When all of these factors are taken into consideration, inclusion happens.

PART II: KNOWLEDGE

KNOWING HOW TO IMPLEMENT INCLUSION

Controversies surrounding inclusion lie in determining how to transform a philosophical position into actual practice. Conflicts in making inclusion-based decisions arise when two groups, typically schools and parents, disagree about *where* a student should be educated—in general education settings or in separate educational settings. Although popular opinion holds that it is often the schools advocating for separate educational settings and parents lobbying for general education settings, this is not always the case. Inclusion too frequently becomes an emotional issue of "Where?—In or Out?" This narrow interpretation of inclusion fails to take the law into consideration and often leaves both groups frustrated and unable to communicate with each other.

Many conflicts potentially could be avoided if the groups did not see where a student is to be educated as superseding other **IEP team** decisions such as what the educational goals are for a student and how that instruction is best implemented. The basic tenets of IDEA provide a framework for making decisions that ultimately serve the best interest of the student and meet the needs and wishes (even the sometimes conflicting ones) of schools and parents.

Understanding IDEA

The focus of the **Individuals with Disabilities Education Act**, most recently reauthorized in 1997, is the same as the focus of the original act authorized in 1975—the provision of an *appropriate education* for students with disabilities. In order to ensure that students with disabilities receive an education tailored to their unique needs, the Act delineates specific considerations aimed at the guarantee of educational benefit. The "Six Principles of IDEA" highlight the steps Congress believes must be taken to ensure that students with disabilities receive an appropriate education (NICHCY, 1999). The six principles are:

- **Free, appropriate public education (FAPE)**—Education should be provided at no cost to the parents, be appropriate to the unique needs of the student, be provided by or paid for by the public education system, and *result in educational benefit for the student.*

- **Appropriate Evaluation**—Evaluations should be conducted by trained personnel. In addition, a variety of instruments and procedures should be used and the evaluations should not be culturally or racially discriminatory. Testing should be conducted in the student's native language.

- **Individualized Education Program (IEP)**—The IEP is a written statement of a student's educational plan. It includes: present levels of performance; measurable annual goals accompanied by short-term or benchmark objectives; a statement of special education and related services and supplemental aids; a statement of the extent to which the student will participate with nondisabled students; and a description of participation in state or district-wide assessments. The IEP team is composed of the parents, at least one special educator, at least one general educator, a representative of the public agency, an individual who can interpret the instructional implications of evaluation results, and any related service personnel.

- **Least Restrictive Environment (LRE)**—To the maximum extent appropriate, school districts are required to educate students with disabilities in general education classrooms with students without disabilities.

- **Parent and Student Participation in Decision Making**— School districts must take steps to ensure that parents and students (when appropriate) are present at each IEP meeting and have the opportunity to participate.

- **Procedural Due Process**—A constitutional guarantee that all legal proceedings will be fair and that one will be given notice of the proceedings and an opportunity to be heard. Parents and schools are guaranteed a hearing by an impartial officer when disagreements occur.

Given these six principles, it is clear that Congress supports placements in general education settings. The primary concern of Congress, however, was and remains the delivery of FAPE, with particular emphasis on the "appropriate education" aspect of FAPE. What constitutes an appropriate education is determined by assessment, input from all members of the IEP team, and the ability (as perceived by the team and/or determined by past experience) for educational benefit to occur.

Defining "educational benefit" can become so complicated as to necessitate court involvement. The Board of Education v. Rowley (458 U. S. 176, 1982) is often cited as a defining FAPE court case. In the Rowley case, the school denied the parents' request for a sign-language interpreter for their daughter, Amy, who was hard of hearing. The school provided Amy with an FM monitor in order to make use of her residual hearing by amplifying sounds as well as provided her with speech and language supports. The school based its decision on Amy's prior experience with an interpreter that occurred for a two-week trial period the year before. The interpreter, in working with Amy, had decided that she could progress without the services. Although Amy was not hearing as much as the other students in her class and therefore was potentially missing some instruction, the school determined that what she was missing did not substantially limit her ability to benefit from the placement without an interpreter. The district court, in finding for the school, found that: "evidence firmly establishes that Amy is receiving an 'adequate' education, since she performs better than the average child in her class and is advancing easily from grade to grade" (483 F Supp., at 534). The Supreme Court upheld the lower court's decision. Thus, the educational benefit clause of IDEA means that students should be making more than trivial progress towards IEP goals, but it does not mean the education must "maximize" students' potential.

Some view inclusion to be a battle between the FAPE principle and the LRE principle. However, in sorting out LRE court cases, the courts consider the appropriateness of the education (FAPE) as having precedence over the placement in which that education occurs (LRE). That is, the courts support LRE decisions in which schools determined *how* education is best delivered before determining *where* the student should be educated (Crockett & Kauffman, 1999).

To embrace both the spirit of IDEA, which is at its heart pro-inclusion, and the letter of the law, which balances placement decisions with the larger "appropriate education" mandate, IEP teams should take into consideration the following to guide them in making final placement decisions:

- the educational goals of the student as determined collaboratively by the IEP team;

- which special education and related services are necessary to support the IEP-determined educational goals; and

- an examination of larger social and educational issues inherent to the educational environment.

Educational Goals

A student's educational goals are determined at an IEP meeting. The goals should be based upon the assessment data collected, input from IEP team members, and a review of the general education curriculum. Goals can be written for academic, social, communication, physical, and/or emotional domains.

Assessment data may include student scores on standardized tests such as IQ or achievement tests, teacher/parent rating scales, specialized assessments from related service personnel (e.g., **speech-language pathologists**, psychologist, **occupational therapists**), or classroom observation notes. Assessment data are reported as "present levels of performance" and serve as a baseline for making decisions regarding annual goals.

Based upon assessment data, IEP team members will have individual views on what constitutes an appropriate education for the student. In many cases, IEP team members will be in consensus about what the long-term aims for a student should be and the short-term steps necessary to facilitate those long-term plans. In some cases, however, teams will need to present their ideas and negotiate a vision for the education of that student. One area of conflict that can arise during goal setting is determining what is reasonable for a student to accomplish in one year. For example, a parent may believe a student can achieve a certain reading level or behavioral goal in one year's time, while the special education teacher may feel the goal is too ambitious. In these cases, the members should refer to the student's present level of performance, discuss past performance and growth, and consider new supports that will be in place to facilitate student progress.

Since the reauthorization process of IDEA in 1997, IEP goals should also be determined with the general education curriculum in mind. In other words, how students will progress in general education curriculum should be emphasized in IEP goals when appropriate. During the reauthorization process, Congress hoped to increase accountability and expectations for students with disabilities. One avenue for increasing standards for students with disabilities was to make sure that IEP teams kept an eye on what was happening in the general education curriculum.

IEP goals consist of annual goals and short-term objectives. **Annual goals** are the IEP team's estimate of what a student can accomplish in one year. These broad goals are written for each area of identified student need. For some students, these goals may be written primarily for academic areas (e.g., reading, math, problem solving); for other students, the goals may focus on specific behaviors or functional skills (e.g., initiating a conversation, brushing one's teeth, expressing anger in an appropriate manner). According to IDEA 1997 all annual goals must:

- be measurable;
- include what the student can reasonably accomplish in one year;
- relate to how the student can progress in the general education curriculum and/or address other educational needs related to the disability; and
- be accompanied by short-term objectives. (Gibb & Dyches, 2000)

Depending upon the number of identified areas of need, the number of annual goals will vary. The average range can be from as few as two goals to as many as ten (Disability Rights Center, 2002).

Each annual goal is broken down into short-term objectives. **Short-term objectives** are the list of steps or sub-skills needed to be met in order to realize the annual goal. A statement to how those objectives will be measured and reported to parents should also be included. Refer to the box "A Closer Look: Annual Goals and Short-Term Objectives" for examples of what annual goals and short-term objectives a team may select for a student.

A Closer Look   **Annual Goals and Short-Term Objectives**

A general guideline for writing annual goals and short-term objectives is to include a description of the behavior, the conditions under which it needs to be met, and the criterion for mastery.

Below are examples of annual goals and accompanying short-term objectives that meet these requirements.

- Martha will increase her reading fluency to 60 words per minute (wpm) at the 2.5 reading level.

    - Given a 2.0 reading level passage, Martha will orally read the passage with at least 98% accuracy at a 60 wpm rate.

    - Given a 2.5 reading level passage, Martha will orally read the passage with at least 98% accuracy at a 60 wpm rate.

- Matthew will be able to compute correct change from $100 when given up to three items totaling less than $100.

    - Given $10, Matthew will be able to correctly compute the change when given one item with 100% accuracy for 3 consecutive trials.

    - Given $50 and a calculator, Matthew will be able to correctly compute the change given 2 items with 100% accuracy for 3 consecutive trials.

    - Given $100 and a calculator, Matthew will be able to correctly compute the change for three items with 100% accuracy for 3 consecutive trials.

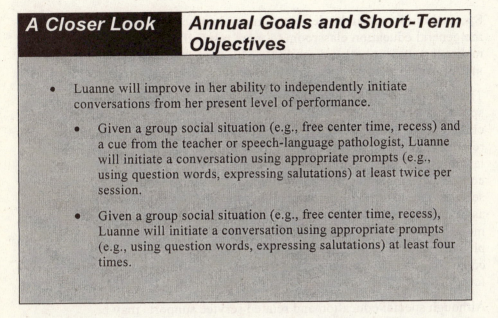

| A Closer Look | Annual Goals and Short-Term Objectives |

- Luanne will improve in her ability to independently initiate conversations from her present level of performance.

  - Given a group social situation (e.g., free center time, recess) and a cue from the teacher or speech-language pathologist, Luanne will initiate a conversation using appropriate prompts (e.g., using question words, expressing salutations) at least twice per session.

  - Given a group social situation (e.g., free center time, recess), Luanne will initiate a conversation using appropriate prompts (e.g., using question words, expressing salutations) at least four times.

Given the type of goals an IEP team may create for a student, placement determinations may be evident. For example, if one of the annual goals is for the student to improve his or her social skills, placement in a general education setting for at least part of the day may be an important part of facilitating the student's attaining that goal. Interacting with peers without disabilities and observing appropriate social interactions could be part of the team's plan for goal achievement. As goals are determined, the team members may discuss which placements would better support which goals.

Special Education and Related Services

Once annual goals and short-term objectives are established for a student, the team must determine which special education and related services might be required to support the student in meeting the agreed upon goals. It is important to remember that "special education" is not a place, but a service. Specifically, **special education** is instruction that is designed to meet the unique needs of a student with a disability. The difference between special education and general education is that in special education the unit of focus is the individual student's IEP goals and in general education the unit of focus is the grade level curriculum.

Special education can be delivered in any instructional setting—from the general education classroom to more restrictive settings. What makes the student with a disability's education "special" is the instructional modifications, **related services**, and/or supports received.

The law requires that each student's IEP include a "statement of the specific special education and related services to be provided to the child and the extent to which the child will be able to participate in regular education programs" (34 CFR §300.346 (a) (3)). Although the law does not specifically define or delineate which services are considered supplemental, common special education and related services include: modifications to the general education curriculum, assistance of an itinerant teacher with special education training (e.g., a mobility instructor), use of computer-assisted devices, occupational and physical therapy, interpreter services, transportation, guide services, counseling, nursing services, and the use of a resource room to name a few.

Although special education and related service supports may be necessary regardless of the place in which the student could be educated, placement discussions typically play a part in determining special education and related services. For example, a student who is behind two reading levels may require intensive reading support that is significantly different than the reading instruction delivered in the general education setting. The most appropriate place for the student to receive this "special education" may be the resource room. Similar to when establishing educational goals, IEP teams should consider how placement will affect the services the student will receive.

Educational Environment

The final point of consideration is the educational environment. When making placement determinations, the IEP team should also take into consideration the impact the student with the disability will have within the general education environment. The following factors should guide this type of decision-making:

- the educational benefit to the student from the general education environment in comparison to the benefits of special education served in more restrictive environments;

- the benefit to the student with a disability from interacting with students without disabilities; and

- the degree of disruption of the education of other students resulting in the inability to meet the unique needs of the student with a disability.

These broader factors can be the most challenging for IEP teams to address. In balancing the social and academic benefits issue, teams consider the unique goals established for the student and then determine the priority of those goals in light of the benefits that could occur in the various placement options.

INCLUSION AND THE DECISION-MAKING PROCESS

In summary, IDEA spells out considerations at each step that supports inclusion-based thinking and decision-making. When determining and writing annual goals, teams need to consider a student's progress in the general education curriculum. When determining special education and related services, teams must include a statement that describes the student's level of participation general education settings. When evaluating the overall educational environment of a student with a disability, teams must consider the potential benefits the student may have on students without disabilities and vice versa. Although teams may decide the general education curriculum is not an appropriate marker for a student or that more restrictive settings would best suit a student's needs, the process is designed to encourage placement in less restrictive environments whenever possible.

By following the previously described decision making steps, IEP teams follow both the spirit and letter of the law. There are certain factors, however, that are illegal for the IEP teams to base their placement decisions. They are:

- the category of disability alone ("*All* students with mental retardation will be placed in self-contained settings");

- the configuration of the current delivery system ("The school system currently offers placement in *either* the general education classrooms or in self-contained classrooms.

Therefore, students will be placed in one or the other setting and the continuum of placement alternative is not available");

- the availability of educational or related services ("There is no speech-language pathologist available and therefore, no student will receive speech-language services");

- the availability of space ("The self-contained class for students with emotional or behavioral disorders is full and therefore, the student will remain in the general education setting"); and

- administrative convenience—("Scheduling would be easiest if all students with disabilities were placed in general education classes").

Obviously, these factors do not embrace the individualized nature of the special education process. As schools and districts move towards pro-inclusion models, the essence of special education remains the preservation of an appropriate education based upon the unique needs of individual students. Inclusion reminds educators to keep standards/expectations high and an eye towards the larger social goals of education. Inclusion is not meant to restrict options for students with disabilities.

PART III: APPLICATIONS

KEYS TO SUCCESSFUL INCLUSION

Students with disabilities who are placed in less restrictive environments will not automatically thrive simply given close proximity to peers without disabilities or by being *exposed to* general education instruction. Successful inclusion must be rooted in effective collaboration between special and general educators and differentiated teaching practices.

Collaboration

Friend and Bursuck (1999) define **collaboration** as "a style of interaction professionals use in order to accomplish a goal they share" (p. 486). This definition captures the essence of collaboration—a specific way of working together to meet a shared goal. Teachers can be on the same grade-level team or even teach in the same room and not collaborate. Collaboration occurs when all parties actively participate or have the opportunity to participate in the planning or implementation of a task. Collaboration takes considerable work and may be the greatest challenge to successful inclusion.

Historically, the teaching profession is marked by isolation. The autonomous nature of teaching serves as a double-edged sword for many—the freedom to teach and interact with students and yet the loneliness of working without a clear support structure. In recent years, the movement towards fostering greater interaction among teachers has been gaining momentum (Friend & Bursuck, 1999). At the elementary level, increasing numbers of teachers work in grade level teams. At the middle school level, teachers are frequently working in interdisciplinary teams. At the high school level, content area departments have developed structures of interdependence and problem solving.

Although the nature of teaching and the social structure of schools are changing, many teachers find the process of working with others a daunting and challenging task. Working closely with colleagues demands a different set of skills from those required to teach students.

These skills can include: balancing educational perspectives, negotiating instructional territory, determining alternative teaching roles, and sharing professional responsibilities and outcomes, to name a few. Successful inclusion practices necessitate that teachers work together in collaborative relationships. In response to the challenges inherent to teaming relationships, various guidelines for developing collaborative relationships have been established (Cook & Friend, 1995; Friend & Bursuck, 1999; Pugach & Johnson, 2002; Wood, 2002). Many of the guidelines can be narrowed down to two key components—clear communication and a plan for negotiating territory.

Communication

One of the biggest challenges to collaboration is communication. Teachers are busy and have many demands placed upon them. Thus, they often fall into poor communication habits (e.g., not listening, rushed sharing of information, quick judgments). These failures to communicate may result in teachers working in isolation or even against each other in trying to meet the needs of students with disabilities. Feelings of hostility or ill-will can also result.

To avoid breakdowns in communication, teachers should plan for communication opportunities. Particularly in the early stages of collaboration building, teachers need to spend time talking, listening, and developing a system for sharing information and responsibilities. Investing this time up front will pave the way for open communication as conflicts or challenges arise during the course of the year.

Refer to the box "Practical Tips and Strategies: Foundations and Barriers to Effective Communication" for more information about avoiding communication traps and developing strong communication strategies.

Practical Tips and Strategies | Foundations and Barriers to Effective Communication

Pugach and Johnson (2002) identify the following communication skills as foundational for successful collaboration:

- Listen and provide feedback on what you felt the speaker was saying by restating key information.

- Offer support by allowing appropriate time to communicate (i.e., not in the hallway or running to an IEP meeting).

- Create space for the other person to share information through general opening statements such as "How are things going in your class?" rather than "I heard you were experiencing some difficulties; tell me about them."

- State the implied message of the speaker by stating what their body language communicates or what you interpret from reading into what they are saying. For example, a colleague who tells you everything is okay but is slouched over and mumbles the words is communicating an implied message of frustration or being overwhelmed.

Equally important to using effective communication skills is avoiding communication barriers. Pugach and Johnson (2002) offer the following list of common barriers:

- Offering advice before fully assessing a situation or with the expectation that the colleague needs to follow-through on the advice.

- Providing false reassurances such as "Everything will work out" or "You will be fine." False reassurances serve to either dismiss the significance of the issue or minimize the colleague's power to change the situation.

- Asking misdirected questions—too many questions at one time or questions that do not serve a common purpose.

- Interrupting or changing the subject when the colleague is speaking.

- Responding to the situation or concern presented with clichés.

Negotiating Territory

If open communication is the first step towards successful collaboration, negotiating responsibilities comprises the rest of the journey. Teachers grapple with questions like: What instructional role will I play in this classroom? Who will be responsible for grading? Will "my students" become "our students" and how will that happen? These issues often plague teachers who are about to embark on a collaborative relationship.

Prior to dividing responsibilities, teachers should clarify their positions on topics such as instructional beliefs, approaches to instructional planning, preferred routines, discipline strategies, and pet peeves (Cook & Friend, 1995). Discussing these matters prior to actual instruction increases the chances that differences can be amicably addressed before they become major issues. Conversely, if teachers find that their fundamental beliefs about teaching are not compatible they are likely to encounter difficulty regardless of communication efforts!

Once teachers are aware of each other's instructional philosophies, they can begin to plan their specific roles in the relationship. In some cases teachers will be involved in collaborative consultation and in other cases teachers will be involved in collaborative teaching (co-teaching). **Collaborative consultation** occurs when the general educator and the special educator jointly plan for the instruction of a student with a disability. In many cases of collaborative consultation the teachers will not team-teach but designate what their individual responsibilities will be and how those responsibilities will serve to support each other albeit in different settings. For example, a student with a disability may spend the majority of the day in the general education setting and receive pullout services for mathematics. The general educator and special educator will collaborate to determine the instructional strategies the general educator should use when teaching the student in the general education classroom and what support services the special educator needs to provide when working with the student in the pullout setting. Even though the teachers are not teaching together, the success of the student is dependent upon this collaborative consultation.

Collaborative or **Co-teaching**, on the other hand, involves a general educator and a special educator delivering substantive instruction to a group of students with diverse needs (Cook & Friend, 1995). In the case of co-teaching, both professionals come together to design a program or schedule of instruction that optimizes their strengths. Co-teaching can take the form of an array of teaching models. Refer to the box "Models of Co-Teaching" for descriptions of various co-teaching arrangements.

Practical Tips and Strategies | Models of Co-Teaching

Over the years many models of co-teaching have been described (Cook & Friend, 1995; Friend & Bursuck, 1999; Wood, 2002). Although specific names for the models may change from author to author, the important thing to keep in mind when reviewing co-teaching models is that no one model will work for all instructional situations or teacher personalities. Co-teaching models should be selected based upon the specific instructional goals for that instructional segment. Seven co-teaching models described by Wood (2002) are:

- **One teach, one observe**—One teacher assumes the primary responsibility for instruction; the other monitors student behaviors.

- **One teach, one drift**—One teacher has primary responsibility for instruction; the other teacher assists students as needed during the instruction (e.g., clarifying instructional points, monitoring behavior, checking work).

- **Station teaching**—Teachers divide instruction into at least two parts; teachers work with small groups of students and then switch groups so that all students receive the same instruction.

- **Parallel teaching**—Each teacher teaches half of the class; each teacher addresses the same material.

- **Remedial teaching**—One teacher reteaches a student or group of students who have not mastered some material; the other teacher works with the rest of the students.

- **Supplemental teaching**—One teacher presents instruction in a modified format for a student or group of students struggling with a topic or skill; the other teacher presents the lesson in the standard format.

- **Team teaching**—Both teachers present the lesson together; one teacher may begin the lesson and the other teacher steps in where appropriate or specific tasks throughout the lesson are designated to the teachers.

In co-teaching arrangements, both teachers share equal responsibility for planning, instructing, and grading. Teachers should discuss their feelings about the various models and plan for which model they will use during specific instructional situations prior to actual teaching. Often, teachers will find that one or two of the models work best for them and the needs of all of their students.

Differentiating Instruction

Ultimately, successful inclusion is dependent upon the type of instruction students receive. Students with disabilities require *special education* regardless of the setting in which they are receiving their education. Specialized instruction and the related services that are individually designed to provide educational benefit must be viable in the placement determined by the team. Therefore, in addition to the co-teaching models, teachers involved in inclusion (both general and special educators) need to determine how the instruction within those models will be delivered in order to meet the educational benefit standard.

Often, inclusive instruction requires differentiation in order to meet the educational benefit standard. **Differentiation** is the modification of instruction to meet the individual needs of a diverse group of students. Teachers can differentiate in terms of content, process, and products in order to meet the diverse needs of students in their classrooms (Tomlinson, 1999). Teaching in a differentiated classroom requires teachers to be responsive to individual student learning. In order to maintain growth among all students, teachers must continually assess learning. Examples of tasks or features of a differentiated classroom include (Tomlinson, 1999):

- A variety of instructional arrangements are used (e.g., homogenous and heterogeneous grouping; individual, small, and whole class grouping; independent, peer, and collaborative grouping)

- Pacing of instruction varies from topic to topic and even student to student (e.g., some students may require more direct instruction, examples, practice opportunities distributed over a longer period of time)

- Assessment is ongoing and diagnostic; instructional decision making is based upon assessments

- The instructional objectives for a lesson or unit may be different for different students or groups of students

- Assignments may vary according to students to groups of students

- Achievement is defined by measuring individual student growth

- Activities, learning materials, or products are appropriate to students' reading levels, background knowledge or prior experiences, or processing abilities

- Instruction varies from highly structured and concrete to open-ended, process learning depending upon individual instructional objectives and student need

To ensure student growth, teachers must plan for instructional modifications that include consideration of three elements—student characteristics, general education curriculum, and IEP goals. Refer to the box "INCLUDE Strategy: Understanding Reasonable Accommodations" for examples of how teachers can balance the three elements when determining accommodations.

Practical Tips and Strategies	INCLUDE Strategy: Understanding Reasonable Accommodations

Friend and Bursuck (1999) created the INCLUDE strategy for a systematic approach to determining reasonable **accommodations** for students with disabilities.

- Identify classroom environmental, curricular, and instructional demands.

  - Classroom Organization—The ways in which a teacher arranges the physical environment, classroom routines, climate of instruction and interactions, behavior management (e.g., rules

Practical Tips and Strategies	**INCLUDE Strategy: Understanding Reasonable Accommodations**

and rewards system), and use of instructional and non-instructional time falls under the category of classroom organization. Each of these aspects can be considered when making reasonable accommodations. For example, a student may benefit from fewer transitions or from increased structure for receiving and turning in assignments. Each factor of classroom organization has the potential to be modified in some way to support student need.

- Classroom Grouping—At different times during instruction, a teacher may employ different grouping arrangements. Grouping arrangements can vary from whole class, small group (homogeneous—same ability or interest level), small group (heterogeneous—mixed ability or interests), one-to-one, or partner work/cooperative groups. Teachers can view instructional grouping as a reasonable accommodation. For example, after whole-class instruction, teachers can plan for reteaching or reinforcement of the concepts through small, homogeneous grouping for select students.

- Instructional Materials—Instructional materials include content area or skill-based area (reading or math) textbooks, trade books or decodable texts, and media (e.g., films, laser discs, overhead transparencies, software). Student ability to access to instructional materials will have a large impact on their ability to be successful. Materials should be selected with students' reading level, background knowledge, physical dexterity, and organizational skills in mind. Examples of accommodations may include a study guide to assist students in navigating dense textbooks or alternative texts that cover the same material at a lower reading level.

- Instructional Methods—One of the most important and overlooked ways teachers can accommodate students with special needs is to evaluate the ways in which content and skills are taught. Organization, clarity or focus of instructional objectives, opportunities for students to actively participate, and evaluation approaches and frequency of student evaluation are all areas that can be examined when evaluating the effectiveness of instructional methods on student learning. For many students

Practical Tips and Strategies	INCLUDE Strategy: Understanding Reasonable Accommodations

with special needs, instruction needs to be direct, explicit, and systematic to ensure student success.

- **N**ote student learning strengths and needs.

  - Academics—Accommodations for academic needs may include remediating foundational basic skills (reading and math), teaching cognitive strategies for learning content area information, or teaching functional skills.

  - Social/Emotional Development—Students' social emotional development can include their conduct, interpersonal skills, or psychological adjustment. Modifications in this area range from establishing specific behavioral plans to providing social skills training or counseling.

  - Physical Development—The physical needs of a student may necessitate the support of assistive technology (e.g., a FM monitor, large print text), related service personnel, or alternative presentation of classroom instruction.

- **C**heck for potential areas of student successes.

  - Capitalize on areas in which a student has relative strengths. These may be interpersonal, artistic, or a particular subject interest.

- **L**ook for potential problem areas.

  - If a student has an established area of need, instruction and support should be provided for that area. At the same time, however, modifications can be made to reduce the reliance on that deficit area. For example, a student who has difficulty reading may require that all content area tests be read to him. Thus, although he is receiving targeted reading instruction to remediate his difficulties in reading, an accommodation can be made to "by-pass" this weakness in order to get a more accurate view of his content knowledge.

- **U**se information gathered to brainstorm instructional adaptations.

  - Brainstorming should include specifying instructional approaches, strategies to be taught, modifications to assessment

Practical Tips and Strategies	**INCLUDE Strategy: Understanding Reasonable Accommodations**

and assignments, and most importantly, specific skills to be addressed.

- **D**ecide which adaptations to implement.

  - Accommodations should be selected based upon age-appropriateness, easy of implementation, and the demonstrated effectiveness (i.e., avoid fads or unvalidated practices.)

- **E**valuate student progress.

Friend, M., & Bursuck, W. D. (1999). *Including Students with Special Needs: A Practical Guide for Classroom Teachers.* Boston, MA: Allyn and Bacon.

Final Suggestions for Implementing Inclusion

In conclusion, the inclusion of students with disabilities is not an easy task. Professionals engaging in the process of moving towards more inclusive practices should prepare themselves for the complexity and challenge inherent to the process. Teachers, both special and general, will require support in order to meet the new expectations demanded of them. Professional development in the areas of collaboration and designing effective inclusive instruction must be an integral part of any school or district's plan for inclusion.

Some final guidelines for implementing inclusion practices in schools or districts are provided in box: "Guidelines for Implementing Inclusion Policies." These summative points will ensure that schools striving for best practices in the education of students with disabilities will meet the high standards established under IDEA.

Practical Tips and Strategies

Guidelines for Implementing Inclusion Policies

Schools or districts considering moving to more inclusive delivery models should keep in mind the following recommendations:

- Avoid top-down, mandated full inclusion; mandatory full inclusion is contrary to special education law.

- Maintain a continuum of placements, supports, and services, but start with all students' default placement as general education.

- Make placement decisions based upon well-developed IEPs; the educational goals established for individual students should guide the team in determining the setting where those needs can be met.

- Involve all teachers in the decision-making process; collaboration can be challenging and antithetical to traditional teaching processes.

- Provide ongoing staff development related to the unique challenges of inclusion including: team teaching, student grouping, behavior management, student evaluation, etc.

- Ensure that a sufficient number of licensed support staff is available to meet the range of needs of special education students—social, emotional, and cognitive.

PART IV: EXTENSIONS

RESOURCES ON INCLUSION

A great deal has been written on the topic of inclusion. The best way to proceed in your study of inclusion is to consult a variety of resources. Gather resources that present the information from a variety of viewpoints—parents, district administrators, students, university professionals, national organizations, etc. Keep an open mind as you read about how various groups address the issue of how best to include students with disabilities; then, frame the issue within the context of IDEA standards and your community.

BOOKS

Crockett, J. B., & Kauffman, J. M. (1999). *The Least Restrictive Environment: Its Origins and Interpretations in Special Education.* Mahwah, NJ: Lawrence Erlbaum Associates.

National Information Center for Children and Youth with Disabilities (1999). *Individualized Education Programs: LG2 (4th edition).* Washington, D.C.: Author.

Friend, M., & Bursuck, W. D. (1999). *Including Students with Special Needs: A Practical Guide for Classroom Teachers.* Boston, MA: Allyn and Bacon.

Fullan, M., & Hargreaves, A. (1991). *What's worth fighting for? Working together for your school.* Toronto, Ontario: Ontario Public School Teachers.

Henley, M., Ramsey, R. S., & Algozzine, R. F. (2002). *Characteristics of and Strategies for Teaching Students with Mild Disabilities (4th ed.).*

Stainback, S., & Stainback, W. (1996). *Inclusion: A Guide for Educators.* Baltimore, MD: Brookes.

Tomlinson, C. A. (1999). *The Differentiated Classroom: Responding to the Needs of All Learners.* Alexandria, VA: Association for Supervision and Curriculum Development.

ARTICLES

Cook, M. A. (2002). Outcomes: Where are we now? The efficacy of differential placement and the effectiveness of current practices. *Preventing School Failure, 42(2),* 54-56.

Huber, K. D., Rosenfeld, J. G., & Fiorello, C. A. (2001). The differential impact of inclusion and inclusive practices on high, average, and low achieving general education students. *Psychology in the Schools, 36,* 497-504.

Klingner, J. K., Vaughn, S., Hughes, M. T., Schuum, J. S., & Elbaum, B. (1998). Outcomes for students with and without learning disabilities in inclusive classrooms. *Learning Disabilities Research and Practice, 13,* 153-161.

McLeskey, J., & Waldron, N. L. (2002). Inclusion and school change: Teacher perceptions regarding curricular and instructional adaptations. *Teacher Education and Special Education, 25(1),* 41-54.

Vaughn, S., & Klingner, J. K. (1998). Students' perceptions of inclusion and resource rooms. *The Journal of Special Education, 32(2),*79-88.

Voltz, D., Brazil, N., & Ford, A. (2001). What matters most in inclusive education: A practical guide for moving forward. *Intervention in School and Clinic, 37,* 23-30.

Wolpert, G. (2001). What general educators have to say about successfully including students with down syndrome in their classes. *Journal of Research in Childhood Education, 16(1),* 28-28.

WEBSITES

The Center for Effective Collaboration and Practice
http://cecp.air.org/
The mission of the Center is to help communities promote emotional well-being, effective instruction, and safe learning for children and youth with emotional and behavioral problems.

Kids Together, Inc.
http://www.kidstogether.org/

Kids Together, Inc. is a non-profit organization dedicated to providing information and resources to enhance the quality of life for children with disabilities.

Partnerships for Inclusion (PFI)
http://www.fpg.unc.edu/~pfi/
Partnership for Inclusion is a statewide technical assistance grant for North Carolina. PFI provides information to support the inclusion of young children with disabilities, ages birth through five, in all aspects of community life.

TASH
http://www.tash.org/
TASH is an international association of people with disabilities, their family members, other advocates, and professionals fighting for a society in which inclusion of all people in all aspects of society is the norm. (Description from the website.)

Wrightslaw
http://www.wrightslaw.com/
Wrightslaw includes hundreds of articles, cases, newsletters, and resources about special education law and advocacy. Parents, advocates, educators, and attorneys can find accurate, up-to-date information about advocacy for children with disabilities.

VIDEOS

Educating Peter. (1993) (Available from Program Development Associates, 800-543-2119, http://www.pdassoc.com/)

Educating Peter is a documentary of a boy with Down Syndrome and his experiences in an inclusive third grade classroom. The video captures the challenges and rewards both Peter and his classmates experience over the course of the year. This 30-minute documentary highlights many of the complex issues involved in inclusion.

Going To School (Ir a la escuela). (2001) (Available from Richard Cohen Films, PO Box 1012, Venice, CA 90294-1012)

The documentary highlights the lives of three seventh graders and a second grader, revealing the determination of their parents to see that their children receive an equal education in the Los Angeles Unified School District.

Inclusion: Heaven or Hell? (1995) (Available from LRP Publications, 800-341-7874, http://www.lrp.com/)

This 18-minute video elucidates the concept of least restrictive environment (LRE) through real-life examples of LRE cases and litigation. The video offers practical advice on how to design Individualized Education Programs that meet the standards of the law and prevent unnecessary litigation.

Special Needs Students in Regular Classrooms? Sean's Story. (1994) (Available from Films for the Humanities and Sciences, PO Box 2053, Princeton, NJ, 08543)

This documentary presents the story of Sean, an eight-year-old boy with Down Syndrome, and his first year of being included in a general education setting. The film includes a variety of perspectives—teachers who felt unprepared for the challenges of working with a student with a disability to parents (with and without disabilities) who question the appropriateness of the inclusive placement to teachers and parents determined to make inclusion successful. The video also presents a parallel story of Bobby, a boy with Down Syndrome who is being served in a special day school for students with disabilities. Teachers and parents associated with the special day school share their perspectives on why they believe more restrictive settings need to remain an option for students with disabilities.

The Power of 2: Making a Difference through Co-Teaching. The Inclusion Series, Tape 3. (1996) (Available from the Council for Exceptional Children, 888-232-7733, http://www.cec.sped.org/)

This 42-minute video was designed for professional development training for teachers and administrators in elementary and secondary settings to support effective co-teaching practices among special and general educators. Facilitator materials include discussion questions, group activity options, and summary handouts.

PROFESSIONAL ASSOCIATIONS

National Information Center for Children and Youth with Disabilities

P.O. Box 1492
Washington, D.C. 20013-1492
Telephone: 1-800-695-0285

Consortium on Inclusive Schooling Practices

Allegheny Singer Research Institute
320 E. North Avenue
Pittsburgh, PA. 15212
Telephone: (412) 359-1600

California Research Institute on the Integration of Students with Severe Disabilities

San Francisco State University
14 Tapia Drive
San Francisco, California 94132
Telephone: (415) 338-7847

FOR REFLECTION

1. Federal legislation calls for students to be placed in the least restrictive environment (LRE). How is LRE defined and what does LRE mean in terms of placement decisions for students with disabilities?

2. Describe the process courts use in determining where students should be educated.

3. In what ways does a "mainstreaming perspective" differ from an "inclusion perspective"? What are the implications for students with disabilities?

4. Create your own definition of inclusion. Include key components of inclusion as defined by advocacy groups, legislation, practice, etc.

5. List and describe the potential benefits of including a student with a disability into a general education classroom.

6. Describe the relationship between FAPE and LRE.

7. All students with disabilities are required to have a free, appropriate, public education. What factors should schools consider when determining if a student is or will be able to receive an *appropriate education?*

8. How should the annual goals and short-term objectives established for a student with a disability guide placement decision making?

9. All students identified under IDEA are entitled to *special education.* Describe at least five ways in which education in general education settings can be modified in order to meet the definition of special education.

10. For some advocates of inclusion the social benefits of placement in general education settings far outweigh consideration of academic benefits. Under what conditions do you think that social benefits should be given more weight than academic benefits when determining placement for a student?

11. Describe at least two barriers to successful collaboration and strategies teachers can use to overcome these challenges.

12. Review the "Models of Co-Teaching" box on page 22. Select two models to critique. For each model, describe potential benefits and challenges.

13. Friend and Bursuck's (1999) INCLUDE strategy presents an excellent approach to determining reasonable accommodations. Using the INCLUDE strategy, brainstorm as many possible accommodations you think would be viable in a general education setting.

14. Your school is moving towards providing more inclusion options for students with disabilities. You are selected to lead the committee. What guidelines do you think should be instrumental in developing the school-wide plan?

GLOSSARY

accommodations Changes in how a test is administered that do not substantially alter what the test measures; includes changes in presentation format, response format, test setting or test timing; appropriate accommodations are made to provide equal opportunity to demonstrate knowledge.

annual goals Statements of estimated yearly outcomes in a student's identified areas of need.

case law Decisions issued by a court.

collaboration A style of interaction professionals use in order to accomplish a goal they share.

collaborative consultation A general educator and a special educator jointly planning for the instruction of a student with a disability.

collaborative teaching (co-teaching) A general educator and a special educator delivering substantive instruction to a group of students with diverse needs.

continuum of alternative placements The full range of alternative placements, from those assumed to be least restrictive to those considered most restrictive; the continuum ranges from general education classrooms in neighborhood schools to resource rooms, self-contained classes, special day schools, residential or hospital settings, and home instruction.

differentiation The modification of instruction to meet the individual needs of a diverse group of students.

due process hearing Procedures outlined in IDEA for ensuring that parents' and children's rights are protected and for resolving disputes that may arise during the IEP process; administrative hearing before an impartial hearing officer or administrative law judge.

full inclusion All students with disabilities are placed in their neighborhood schools in general education settings for the entire day.

general education settings Classroom or school environments such as the cafeteria and non-academic classes that students without disabilities typically attend.

Individuals with Disabilities Education Act (IDEA)
Landmark 1975 federal law, originally known as the Education for All
Handicapped Children Act, that guaranteed a "free, appropriate public
education" for all students with disabilities. The law has been amended
several times, most recently in 1997.

inclusion   The commitment to educate students with disabilities in
the least restrictive environment.

individualized education program (IEP)   A written educational plan
that specifies a student's current levels of performance, annual goals
accompanied by short-term objectives, educational services to be
provided, the extent to which the student will be included with students
without disabilities, and an assessment schedule; the IEP is prepared by
the IEP team (see **IEP team**).

IEP team   A group composed of the parents, at least one special
educator, at least one general educator, a representative of the public
agency, an individual who can interpret the instructional implications
of evaluation results, and any related service personnel; the purpose of
the IEP team is to generate the individualized education program.

least restrictive environment (LRE)   The most appropriate
educational placement that is closest to general education or
instructional environments for students without disabilities.

mainstreaming   The process of placing students with disabilities into
general education settings for all or part of the day.

modifications   Substantial changes in what a student is expected to
demonstrate; includes changes in instructional level, content, and
performance criteria, may include changes in test form or format;
includes alternate assessments.

occupational therapist   A specialist who provides therapy and
instruction to students with fine motor difficulties.

physical therapist   A specialist who provides therapy and instruction
to students with gross motor difficulties.

resource room   A service arrangement in which special education is
provided to students with disabilities in a setting other than the general
education classroom; typically, the student is placed in the general

education classroom and visits the resource room only for short periods.

related services   Auxiliary services such as psychological, transportation, or physical therapy that support students with disabilities in receiving benefit from special education.

short-term objectives   Description of steps or sub-skills needed to be met in order to achieve the annual goal.

speech-language pathologist   A specialist who serves students with speech and language impairments.

special education   Instruction specifically designed to meet the unique needs of students.

REFERENCES

Boyle, J. R., & Weishaar, M. (2001). *Special Education Law with Cases*. Boston, MA: Allyn and Bacon.

Crockett, J. B., & Kauffman, J. M. (1999). *The Least Restrictive Environment: Its Origins and Interpretations in Special Education*. Mahwah, NJ: Lawrence Erlbaum Associates.

Cook, L., & Friend, M. (1995). Co-teaching: Guidelines for creating effective practices. *Focus on Exceptional Children, 28*(3), 1-16.

Disability Rights Center (accessed, 2002). *Parent's Guide: Civil Rights*. Available online at: http://lawschool.arkdisabilityrights.org/parentguide/1f-iep.htm

Friend, M., & Bursuck, W. D. (1999). *Including Students with Special Needs: A Practical Guide for Classroom Teachers*. Boston, MA: Allyn and Bacon.

Fullan, M., & Hargreaves, A. (1991). *What's worth fighting for? Working together for your school*. Toronto, Ontario: Ontario Public School Teachers.

Gibb, G. S., & Dyches, T. T. (2000). *Guide to Writing Quality Individualized Education Programs: What's Best for Students with Disabilities?* Boston, MA: Allyn and Bacon.

Lewis, R. B., & Doorlag, D. H. (1999). *Teaching Special Students in General Education Classrooms*. Upper Saddle River, NJ: Merrill/Prentice Hall.

National Information Center for Children and Youth with Disabilities (NICHCY) (1997). *Module 4—Six Principles of IDEA*. Washington, D.C.: Office of Special Education Programs, U.S. Department of Education.

Pugach, M. C., & Johsnson, L. J. (2002). *Collaborative Practitioners, Collaborative Schools (2nd ed.)*. Denver, CO: Love.

Wood, J. (2002). *Adapting Instruction to Accommodate Students in Inclusive Settings*. Upper Saddle River, NJ: Merrill/Prentice Hall.